A series of family friendly short walks within the Sheffield boundary

by Reg Hobson

# Sheffield Country Walks

**Reg Hobson**

First published in the United Kingdom by
Arc Publishing 2013



A record of this book is available from the British Library.
Written by Reg Hobson.

ISBN 978-1-906722-28-9

## Dedication

My thanks to my wife Valerie, without whose help this book would not have been written.

# The walks

Walk 1

# Lower Rivelin Valley

**Distance:** 3 Miles

**Approximate Time:** 1½ Hrs

**Parking:** Rails Rd Car Park

**Refreshments:** Rivelin Valley Cafe

**Description:** A nice flat walk beside the river, ideal for children.

**START: Rails Road Car Park.**

Exit the car park and cross the road to the signed footpath. Follow the path and after a few yards take the left fork. Ignoring the paths on your right, continue to the exit on Rivelin Valley Road.

Do not access the road but continue through a yellow barrier and go parallel to river through two gateposts. Eventually you will join another path just past a waterfall. Continue past a green field on the left, cross a small bridge to a path between the goyt and the river. Carry on down some steps and walk past two dams on your left. At the end of the second dam go down some more steps to a crossroad of paths.

Carry straight on, ignoring paths on left and right, and continue down the valley past another dam on your left. You will come to yet another dam which the path circumvents. Follow the path around this and turn right across a bridge, then left taking you alongside the river.

Continue along the path until you reach Rivelin Valley Road. Go up the steps and turn right. After 50yds turn left down the valley at the signpost. After a short distance you will find a junction of paths, go straight on ignoring the path on the right. At the next crossroad of paths turn left, go past the stepping stones on the left. You will eventually come to a long iron bridge next to allotment no. 7.

Cross this to a children's playground and go round it on the right to the café. Why not have a coffee break in the café before retracing your steps almost exactly? The only difference being at the first crossroad of paths you go straight on instead of turning right. This will bring you to Rivelin Valley Road where you retrace your steps back to the start.

*Rails Road car park*

*Childrens playground*

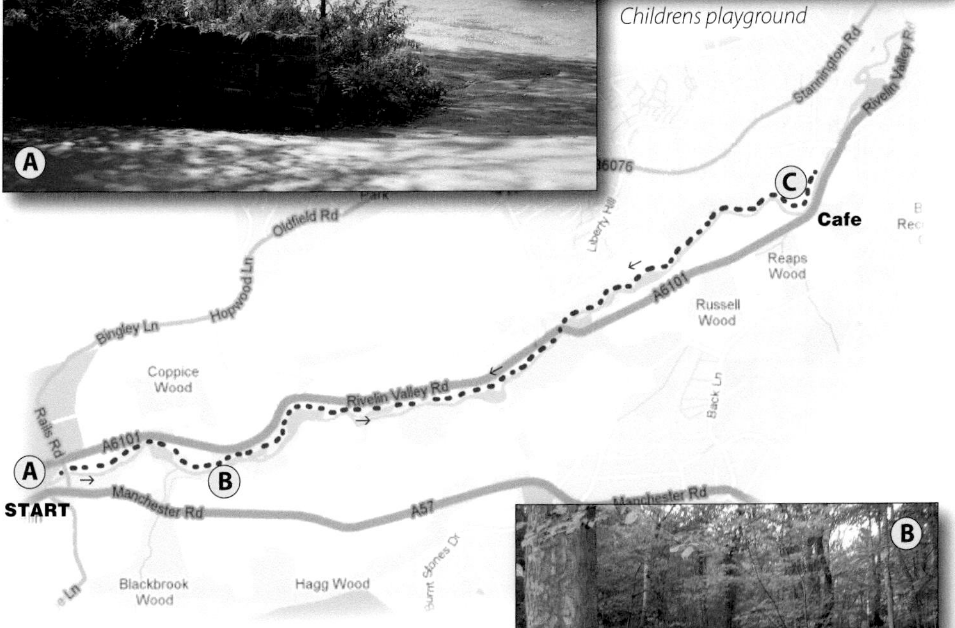

*Stretch of the River Rivelin*

Walk 2

# Lodge Moor Circuit

**Distance:** 3¼ Miles

**Approximate Time:** 1¾ Hrs

**Parking:** Sportsman Pub

**Refreshments:** Shiny Sheff Public House

**Description:** Mostly flat with a steep path down to the brook with the stepping stones.

**START: The Sportsman Public House car park at Lodge Moor.**

Set off from the car park along a vague path at right angles to the road. Walk alongside the football pitch towards a white~topped marker post and continue along the side of the wall to a gravel path.

Turn left and proceed to a road, cross it and go over the stile opposite. Continue left alongside the conduit until you meet Blackbrook Rd, cross it and walk through Spider Park, turning left half way through. The path skirts round a playing field and emerges at Crimicar lane, turn left and continue to the main road (Redmires Road) passing the Shiny Sheff Pub. Cross the main road and walk across the golf course, keeping to the marked path. Over the last fairway the now thin path goes through the trees to a wall. Go through the opening, taking care down the stone steps, turn left and continue steeply downhill to where the path crosses a stream on some large stones.

Cross the stream and veer slightly left and follow the path steeply uphill. At the top turn left and follow the path to a memorial seat in respect of the only known Sheffield victim of the 9/11 disaster in the U.S.A. (There is a fine view from here over Rivelin Valley)

Turn left and continue towards the road (Lodge Lane). Just before the road, fork left, cross the road and go up the path opposite.

Continue on this path to a junction of paths, and take the fork left, carrying on until you reach a T junction where a bridge crosses a stream.

Sportsman Public House, Redmires Road

View from car park over the playing fields

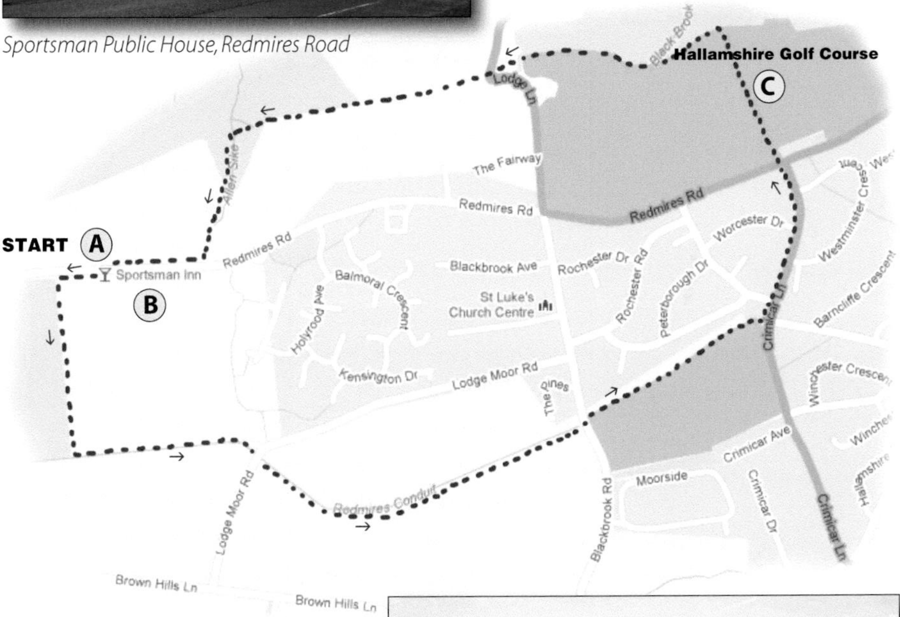


Once over the bridge turn left following the uphill path.

On reaching the main road, turn right and proceed back to the start.

View over Hallamshire Golf Course

Walk 3

# Redmires Dam

**Distance:** 3½ Miles

**Approximate Time:** 1¾Hrs

**Parking:** Redmires Car Park

**Refreshments:** Picnic at Wyming Brook.

**Description:** A variable walk with a climb up Wyming Brook.

**START: Redmires Car Park**

Take the signed path at the side of the car park in a northerly direction away from the road.

Walk through a plantation and then across the moors, crossing a water conduit.

Continue straight on at a crossroad of paths, looking left at the Head Stone –an interesting geological feature.

Carry on down to Rivelin Brook, crossing the bridge and immediately turn right, following the water downstream.

At the next bridge turn right over it and continue along the drive.

Take the left fork and emerge at Rivelin Dam.

At the old, now demolished waterworks building, turn right and climb uphill along Wyming Brook.

Continue to the road and turn right, heading back to the car park.

*View of Redmires top dam from the car park*

*View across Redmires top dam looking towards Stanage Pole.*

*Head Stone*

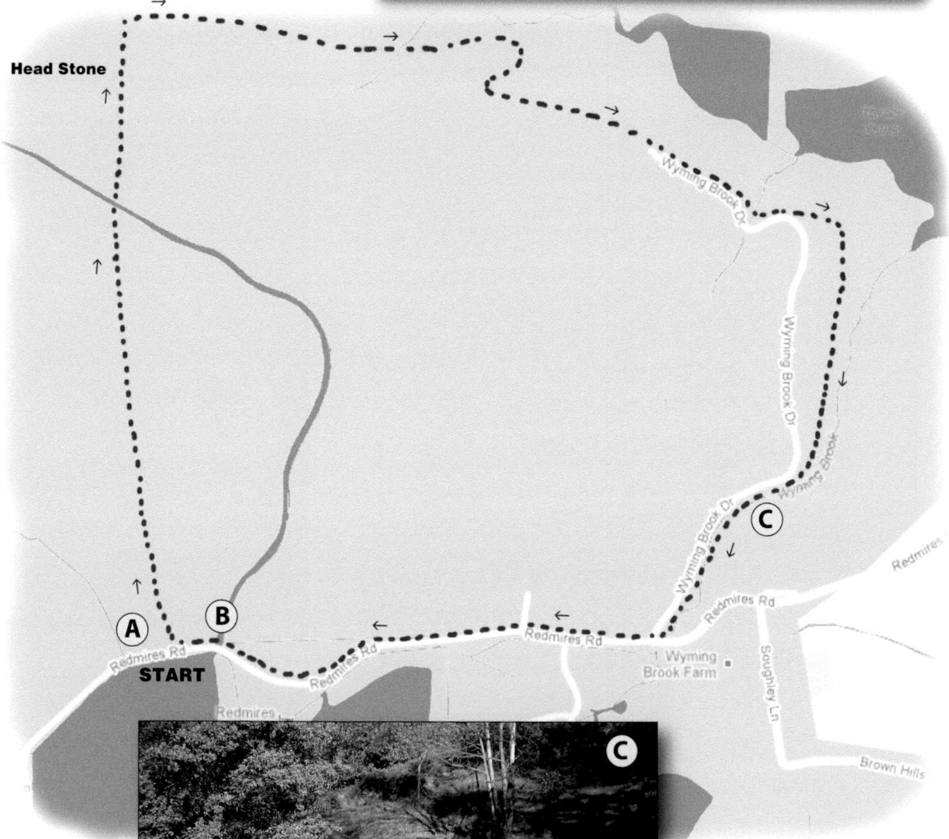

*Stepping stones across Wyming Brook*

Walk
4

# Whitelow Lane (Dore)

**Distance:** 3 Miles
**Approximate Time:** 1½ Hrs
**Parking:** Lay-by on Hathersage Road
**Refreshments:** Door Moor Inn. 1/2 mile towards Sheffield.
**Description:** Pleasant moorland walk.

**START: Top of Whitelow Lane, Dore.**

Walk back towards town and turn left at the signpost (100 yds). Follow the path uphill to the marker post, pausing to see the great view behind you.
Veer left at the post and walk towards the pinnacle of the small hill. Continue to a broken wall, turn right and walk alongside the wall until you reach Houndkirk Road.
Turn left and follow the road to a gate. Turn left and in 10 yds cross the stile on your left. Follow the path diagonally right to the signpost in the corner of the field, cross the stile and turn left.
In 200 yds turn right up Stoney Ridge Road. In 20 yds you will see a lay-by on the left. Fork left at the far end of the lay-by and follow the path. In 150 yds fork left again and then in a further 10 yds fork right towards the far end of a distant plantation. When the path meets a main path at a wall, turn left and walk to a car park.
Turn right, following a path parallel to the main road, continue to a gate and go straight on to what is an entrance from the main road (the Blackamoor Estate).
Do not access the road but continue parallel to it and eventually downhill to a crossroad of paths. Take the left hand path to the Devil's Elbow Gate, continue to Hathersage Road and back to the start.

*Top of Whitelow Lane / Hathersage Road*

*View over Sheffield from Houndkirk Moor*

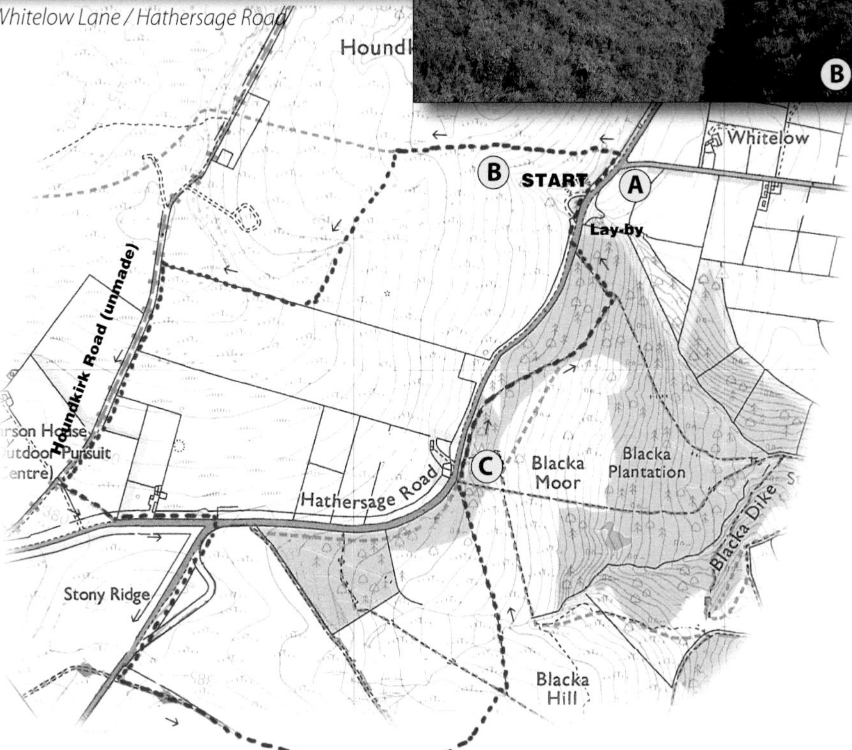

*Path along Blackamoor*

Walk 5

# Ecclesfield

**Distance:** 3 Miles
**Approximate Time:** 1½ Hrs
**Parking:** On Priory Road
**Refreshments:** Picnic
**Description:** A fairly flat walk with variable sights.

**START: Lych Gate on Priory Road at side of Ecclesfield Church.**

Go down Priory Road, turn right and immediately left to walk up to Yew Lane. After the last of the houses on the right hand side, there is a stile in the hedge. Cross it and proceed along the path down the field. Cross the bridge and walk up the gennel to the road.

Turn left and at the side of Town End Farm, turn left again at the signpost and proceed through a gate.

Continue until you hear the brook then cross it and bear right, keeping the hedge and brook on your right.

Continue uphill towards the houses, take the right fork and walk along the leafy path past the houses to the road.

Turn right to the end of the road where diagonally to the right is a signpost which points downhill. Follow this to the stepping stones, cross them and immediately turn right, continuing on this path through a gap in the wall until you reach a lane. Turn right to the Whitley Hall C.C. ground, turning left at the signpost and going through the ground itself and three more fields. In the third field turn sharp left to a stile in the hedge, cross it and proceed straight ahead to a 'hidden path' in the trees at the side of the scrap yard. Follow the path out to a road and turn right.

Continue to a junction and just after this take a side track on the right, uphill and across the field. Walk towards the wooded area until you reach the stone flagged footpath, cross the brook and follow the path past the houses and back to the church.

View over valley

St Mary's Church

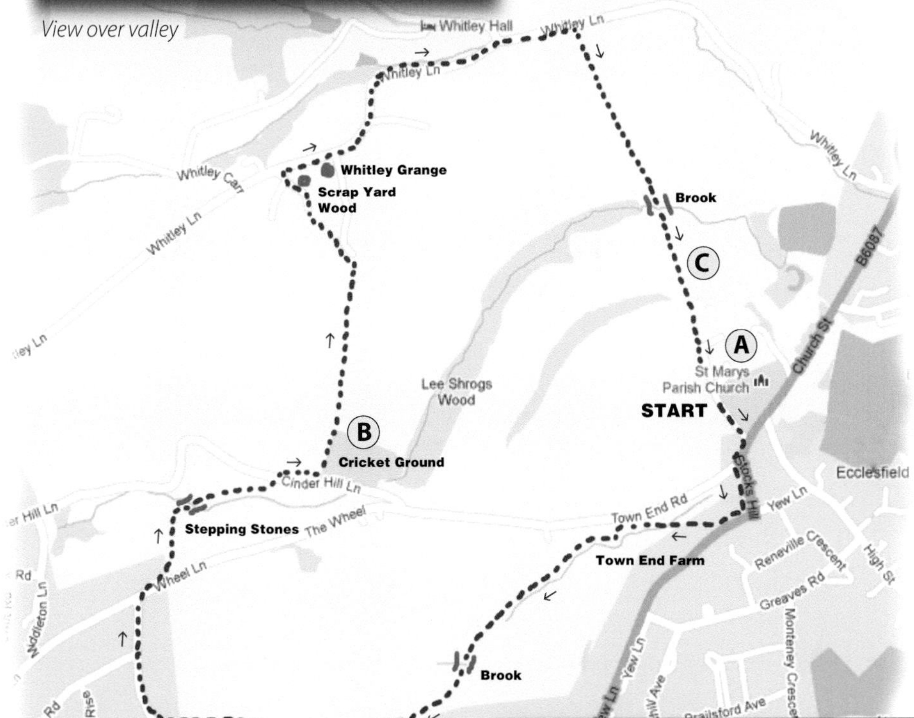

Cricket Pavilion

Walk 6

# Mayfield Valley

**Distance:** 3 Miles

**Approximate Time:** 1½ Hrs

**Parking:** Moorcroft Road

**Refreshments:** Forge Dam Cafe.

**Description:** An easy walk in the Mayfield Valley.

**START: Junction of Hallamshire Road / Crimicar Lane.**

Walk along Moorcroft Road and turn right along the gennel at the side of no. 37. At the top turn left and on reaching Moorcroft Drive turn right. Turn down the gennel at the side of no.25.

On reaching the road turn right, there is a splendid view over Mayfield Valley. At the fork turn left down David Lane to the crossroads.

Go straight across to what was the workhouse area in the olden days, pass some cottages on the right, cross a small bridge and continue to a gate.

Go through this gate and follow the path to a road. Turn left for 20 yds to a signpost on the right, turn right over the stone stile and follow the path at the side of the farm. Cross a ladder stile in a wall and continue through a narrow gap to a junction with a lane.

Turn sharp left here (i.e. down the path alongside the one you've just come along, **not** down the lane).

Cross a small bridge and go to a fork by another bridge.

Take the right fork to a gap in the wall and turn left on the lane. At the next junction go through the hole in the wall at the back of the grass triangle and follow the Public Footpath sign.

Proceed to the junction with a road, cross it and go straight on. Take the left fork over a bridge and walk round the left-hand side of Forge Dam.

Turn left and go down the slope to the café and continue round until you come to a lane (the bottom of Brookhouse Hill).

Turn left for a few yards up the hill to a gap in the wall on the left by a carved stone stating that this is the Forge Valley Path.

Proceed along this path, ignoring side paths, to the junction with School Green Lane and Quiet Lane. Go straight up the former to its junction with Moorcroft Road, turn right and walk back to the start.

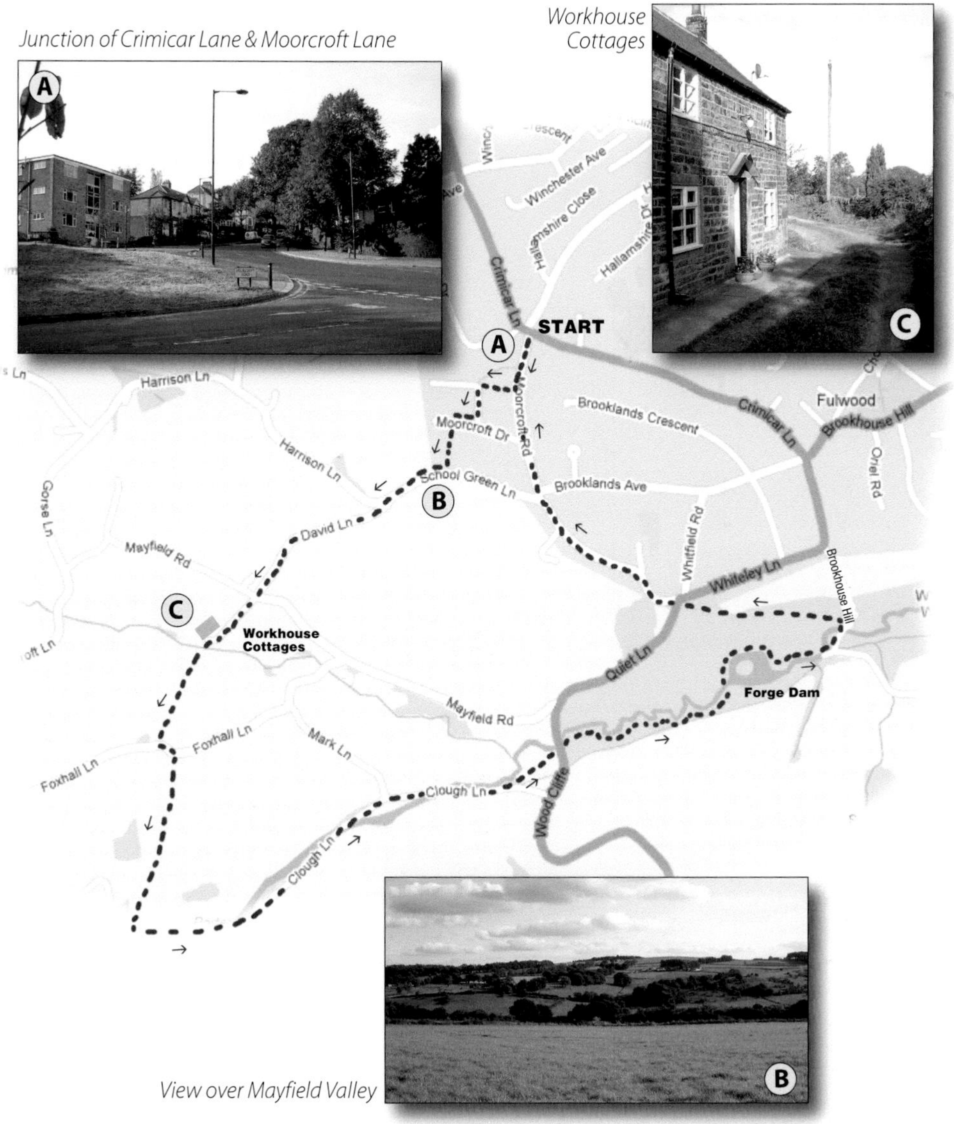


*Junction of Crimicar Lane & Moorcroft Lane*

*Workhouse Cottages*

*View over Mayfield Valley*

Walk 7

# Upper Rivelin Valley

**Distance:** 3 Miles

**Approximate Time:** 1½ Hrs

**Parking:** Rails Road Car Park

**Refreshments:** Picnic

**Description:** This walk has steep paths, both uphill and downhill. The stepping stones often flood after heavy rain.

**START: Rails Road Car Park.**

Cross the road, pass through the opening in the wall and in 20 yards fork right across the bridge.

Turn left and follow the path to the main road (A57). Go straight across and up the drive of Blackbrook Farm (public footpath).

Just inside the gateway veer left across the grass to a stile in the fence, cross it and continue up the hill.

At a junction of paths fork right and walk alongside the wall to a road (Lodge Lane).

Turn left and proceed up the hill to a hairpin bend. Turn right and take the middle one of three paths (the opening is on the right hand side). Continue along this to some stepping stones over a brook. Cross this, turn right and right again on meeting another path.

Walk along to a crossroad of paths where you turn right and proceed downhill (with care) to some steps leading down to some more stepping stones. Cross these and continue to the main road.

Go straight across, over the stile and along the side of the wall to a gateway.

Pass through here and walk diagonally right across the field to a stile in the hedge. Cross this and turn diagonally left to another stile in a hedge. Cross this and a footbridge, turn right and continue to a road.

Turn right again to another road and finally turn right again and walk down to a main road (Rivelin Valley Rd).
Go straight across and back to the start.

*Entrance to Blackbrook Farm*

*View from Lodge lane*

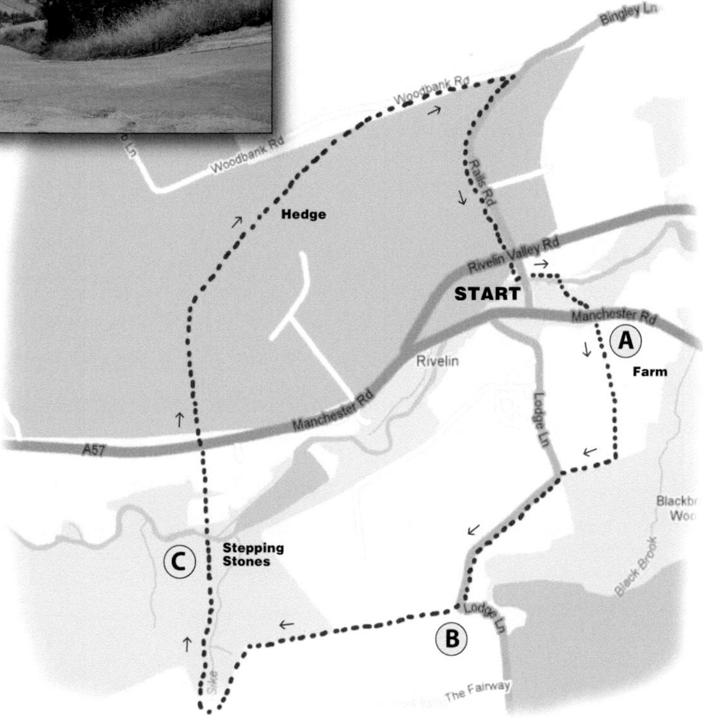

*Stepping Stones*

Walk 8

# Ringinglow

**Distance:** 3¼ Miles
**Approximate Time:** 1¾Hrs
**Parking:** Houndkirk Road.
**Refreshments:** Norfolk Arms, Public House.
**Description:** A pleasant walk around Ringinglow. Little cover if the wind gets up.

**START: The corner of Sheephill Road and Houndkirk Road.**

Walk halfway back to the Round House and turn right at the signpost. Continue on the path to a set of stone flags on end and then to a stile at the top of 'Limb Valley'. Cross this and follow the path uphill to Smeltings Farm. Pass by the farm going over three stiles and arrive at the main road. Turn left for 200 yds to a signpost on the right, turn right and descend into the valley. Cross the stile into a lane and turn left. Turn left again just over the bridge and continue through the woods to a sharp left hand hairpin bend over a bridge. Turn right up some steps to the road. Turn right for 120 yds to a signpost on the left opposite Greenhouse Lane. Turn left at the signpost and continue alongside the wall, forking left to a stile in the fence.

Cross it and follow the path to the left to a stile in the wall. Go over it and turn right, following the path and forking left to the top of the ridge. Follow the path going left to a wooden stile frame and continue downhill to the main road.

Cross the road at the end of Lady Cannings plantation and follow the path down the side of the plantation for 250 yds to a stile on the left opposite a path on the right. Cross the stile and continue along the path to a fork. Here fork left and follow the path, eventually swinging right, to Houndkirk Road and back to the start.

Round House, Ringinglow Village

View across mayfield Valley

View towards the City Centre

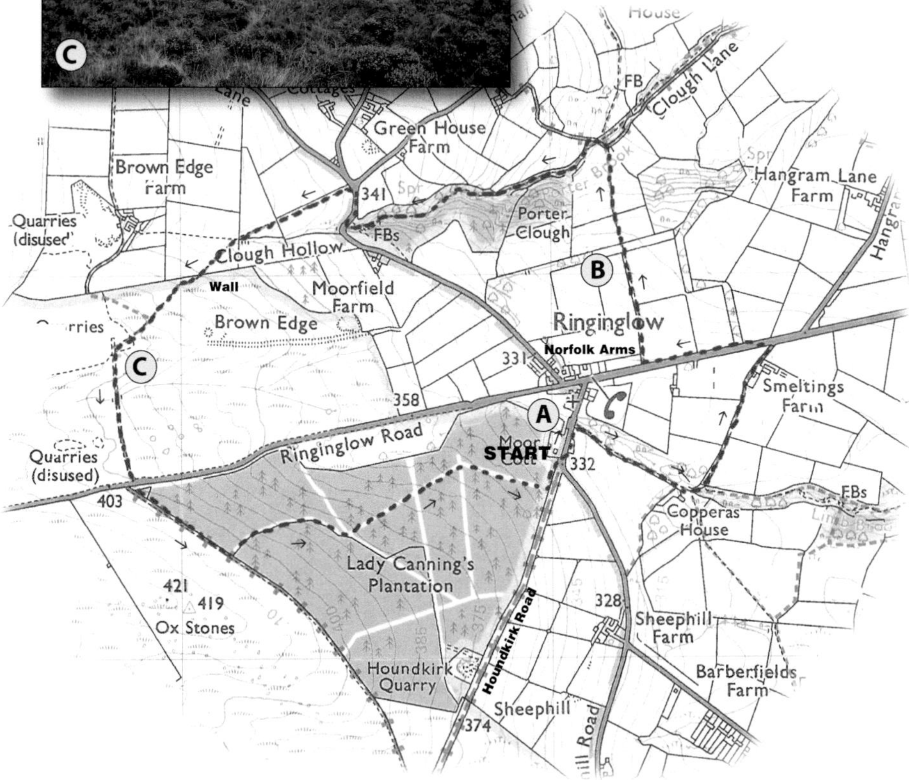

Walk 9

# Beauchief Abbey

**Distance:** 3½ Miles

**Approximate Time:** 1¾Hrs

**Parking:** Beauchief Abbey

**Refreshments:** Castle Inn

**Description:** An interesting variable walk which includes a steep flight of steps.

**START: At the Abbey.**

Walk up Beauchief Abbey Road and turn right at the signpost at the top of the golf course. After a while fork left up a slight incline and continue past Beauchief Hall. Turn right down a few steps then turn left and continue, dropping down right at a signpost.

The path leads to a lot of steps going down to Twentywell Lane, turn right then left across the triangle. Bear left up a small hill and then take the footpath on the right hand side. At the second path take a dog leg turn left to avoid the steep bank. Continue bearing left and then in 300 yds take the left fork to arrive at the Castle Inn.

Turn left then right up Twentywell Lane to a signpost on the left next to house number 285 near the shops. Turn left here and proceed to the Recreation Ground.

Once there turn half left through an opening and proceed across the field to a seat which is in view. This is a splendid place to have a rest, have a picnic or enjoy the glorious view over Dore and Totley and the distant hills.

On again, do not pass through this opening but instead go right and then left at the fork in the corner of the field. Follow the path round the edge of the driving range, turning left at the far end. The path goes downhill and bends to the right at the bottom until it reaches a short flight of steps leading to a farm lane.

Turn left and follow the path between the golf fairways until you come to a metal gate barrier 50 yards past the last of the golf club.

Turn right through a kissing gate. Cross the field and take the second turning on the left and follow the wall down to the Monks' Well (where the Abbey's monks got their water). Climb the stone stile and the bank to the road, turn right and proceed back to the start.

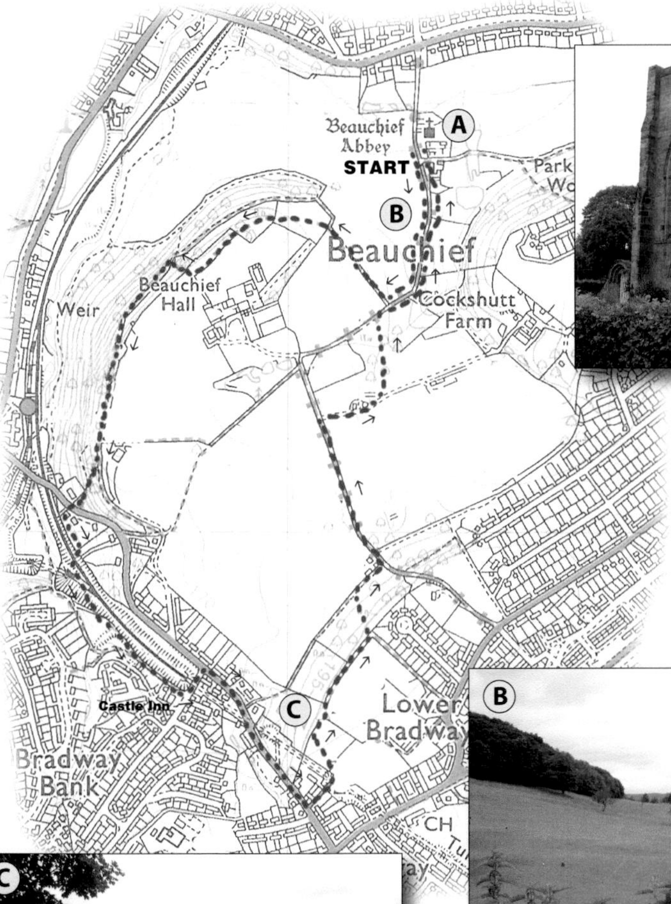

Beauchief Abbey

View over golf course

View over Dore and Totley

Walk 10

# Spider Park

**Distance:** 3½ Miles
**Approximate Time:** 2 Hrs
**Parking:** Hallamshire Road
**Refreshments:** Shiny Sheff
**Description:** Mainly flat but the path down to the river is steep and floods after heavy rain.

**START: Corner of Slayleigh Lane and Hallam Grange Crescent.**

Turn right at the signpost 20 yds along Hallam Grange Crescent and follow the path to a road (Tom Lane) passing Hallam Grange School. Turn left up Tom Lane which forks left immediately and continue uphill via steps and a gennel to Redmires Road and Hallamshire Golf Club. Cross the road, turn left and then in 80 yds turn right at the signpost. Follow the path over the golf course (keeping to the path) between two sets of bollards. At the wall turn left and in 150 yds go through the gap in the wall, turn left and walk 100 yds to a junction of paths and a stream. Turn left and follow the path along the top of the valley, crossing three steep gullies in the process. Eventually the path slopes downhill to another gully and up the other side. Continue on the path steeply downhill to some stone steps across a river. Cross them and veer left steeply uphill, following an indistinct path. Turn left at the top and continue to two seats, where you can rest and note that one of the seats commemorates the only known Sheffield victim of the 9/11 atrocity in America. After resting continue left to Lodge Lane, turn left and walk along it to Redmires Road. Go straight across at the crossroads and walk 600 yds along Blackbrook Road to a signpost on the left.
Turn left and walk along the path through Spider Park to Crimicar Lane.

Turn right and in 100 yds opposite the Sports Pavilion turn left along a gennel which leads to Barncliffe Road. Turn right and in 100 yds turn left into St. Albans Road. Continue for 300 yds along here to another gennel on the left (marked by iron railings). Turn left up the gennel and after 20 yds turn right along a wooded path. Follow it back to the start.

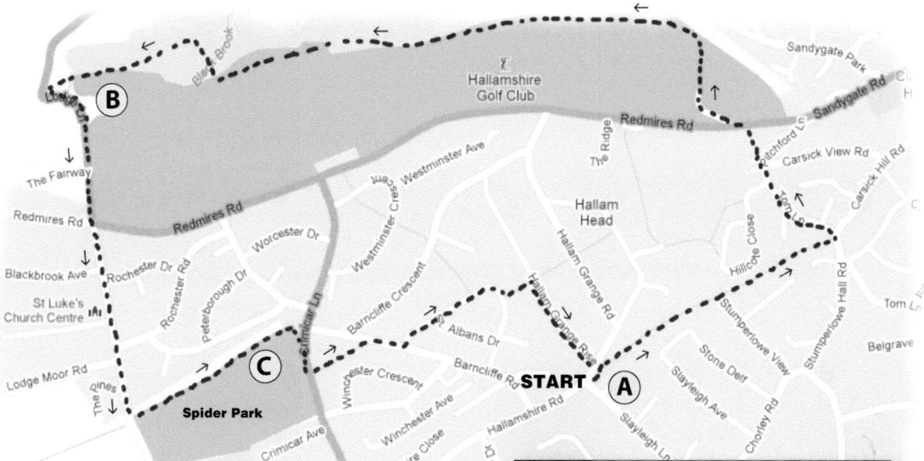

View looking down Slayleigh Lane

9/11 Seat

Spider Park

# Walk 11 Grenoside

**Distance:** 3 Miles
**Approximate Time:** 1½ Hrs
**Parking:** Grenoside Car Park (in woods)
**Refreshments:** Old Red Lion Public House
**Description:** Moderate walk with one steep climb and excellent views.

**START: Car park half a mile past Grenoside village on the left hand side of Woodhead Road.**

Leaving the car park walk left via the signed bridleway on a clear path. After half a mile continue through the barrier at some houses and then straight on down the middle lane.

At the main road (Stephen Lane) turn right and then in 20 yds turn right again up Topside.

After 80 yds turn left up Hill Top Lane and continue to the top where you can admire the great view.

Turn right over the stile, enter the woods and continue to a hard-surfaced bridleway.

Turn left downhill for half a mile until you meet another path.

('T' junction) Turn right and follow it to a junction with a 'complicated' barrier.

Here turn right and proceed uphill, ignoring paths on the right and left.

Eventually this path veers right to a steel barrier gate.

Go through it and back to the start.

Entrance to Warncliffe Woods

Grenoside Car Park

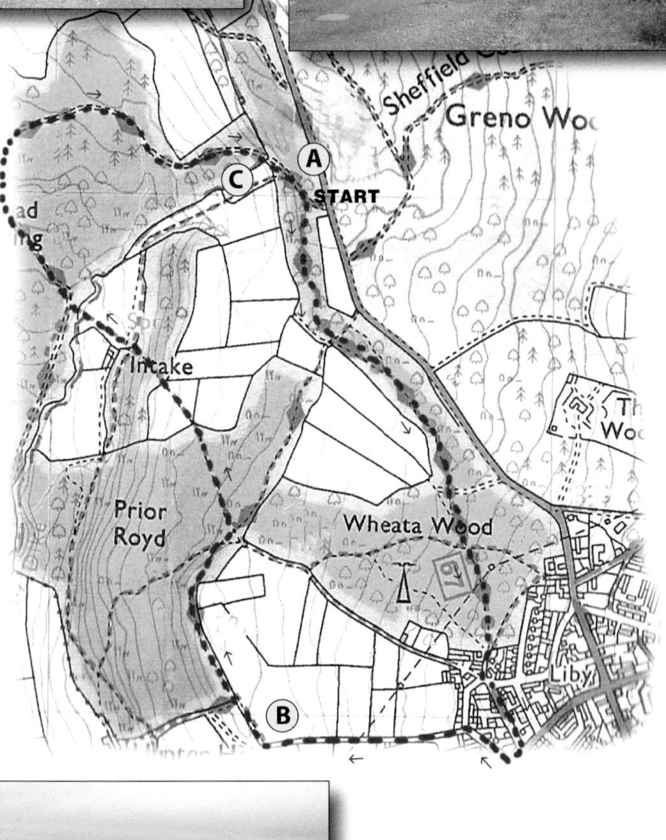

View towards Upper Don Valley

Walk
12

# Whiteley Woods

**Distance:** 3¼ Miles

**Approximate Time:** 1¾Hrs

**Parking:** Brookhouse Hill

**Refreshments:** Forge Dam Cafe.

**Description:** An interesting historic walk around Whiteley Woods.

**START: Junction of Whiteley Lane and Brookhouse Hill.**

Set off down Brookhouse Hill to the junction with Ivy Cottage Lane (on the left before Forge Dam).

Turn left and walk up the lane following the signpost. Continue uphill to the junction with Common Lane where you turn left down Whiteley Wood Road. After 100 yds turn right at the Byway sign.

Walk past the farm and continue uphill to Trap Lane and then at its junction with Muskoka Drive turn left at the signpost.

Walk downhill and fork right after 20 yds, then in another 100 yds turn left down a narrow path.

In another 100 yds veer left and continue downhill. In a further 100 yds turn right and continue straight on at the next junction of paths, eventually coming to a crossroad of paths marked by a post with 4 signs. Here turn right and go up 2 steps (wide apart) and continue on this path to exit at the Highcliffe Road/Greystones Road junction.

Turn diagonally left to walk down the path as signed and after 30 yds veer right along an unmarked path.

After 100 yds at a crossroads of paths carry straight on downhill and then in another 20 yds carry straight on to descend into the valley at Shepherds Wheel.

After crossing the bridge, turn left to another bridge and then follow the path up to the dam. Walk alongside the dam to Hangingwater Road where you turn left and then right at the Peak District sign. In 100 yds fork right and continue to the junction with Whiteley Woods Road. Go straight across and fork left before the stepping stones. Continue on this path to the junction with Brookhouse Hill, turn right and walk back to the start.

*View over Mayfield Valley*

*Corner of Whiteley Lane and Brookhouse Hill*

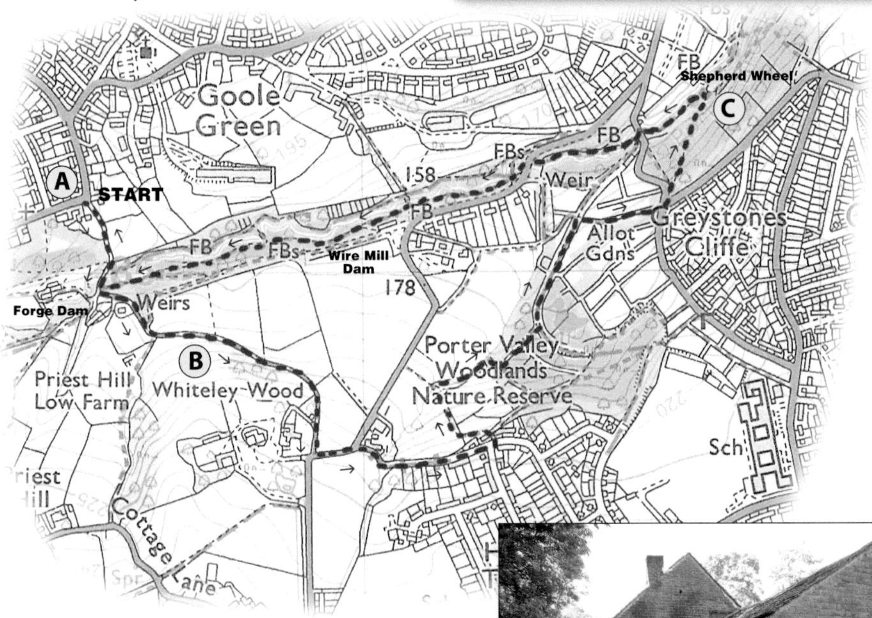

*Shepherd Wheel, a restored working mill which is open to the public*

Walk 13

# Rivelin Valley

## and the Hamlet of Rails

**Distance:** 3 Miles

**Approximate Time:** 1½Hrs

**Parking:** Rails Rd Car Park

**Refreshments:** Picnic

**Description:** Pleasant walk around the Rivelin Valley. Take care walking on the country lanes.

**START: Rails Road car park.**

Leave the car park and turn left, cross Rivelin Valley Road and continue uphill.

The road swings to the right, keep on walking past Bingley Villa on your right hand side to Coppice Lane (a track not a lane) a little further on the right.

There is no road sign here but it is marked by a grass triangle at its start. Turn right here and continue downhill, veering left, to a ladder stile on the left. Cross this and go diagonally across the corner of the field to a stile in the wall. Climb over the stile and proceed on the path through the woods to another stile in the wall on the right.

Go over the stile and walk down to a minor road and then across this to a main road.

Cross the road and go down the railed footpath opposite, to a bridge at the bottom. Cross the bridge and walk uphill along the side of a field, go over the stile and continue up the hill to another stile. Cross it and go upwards again to another two stiles and then a main road.

Cross the road and two more stiles to a wide track. Turn right and follow it to the main road again (Manchester Rd).

Turn left for 20 yards and then turn right down a signed track. Follow this down to Rails Rd and thus back to the start.

*View towards Rails Hamlet*

*View down Coppice Lane*

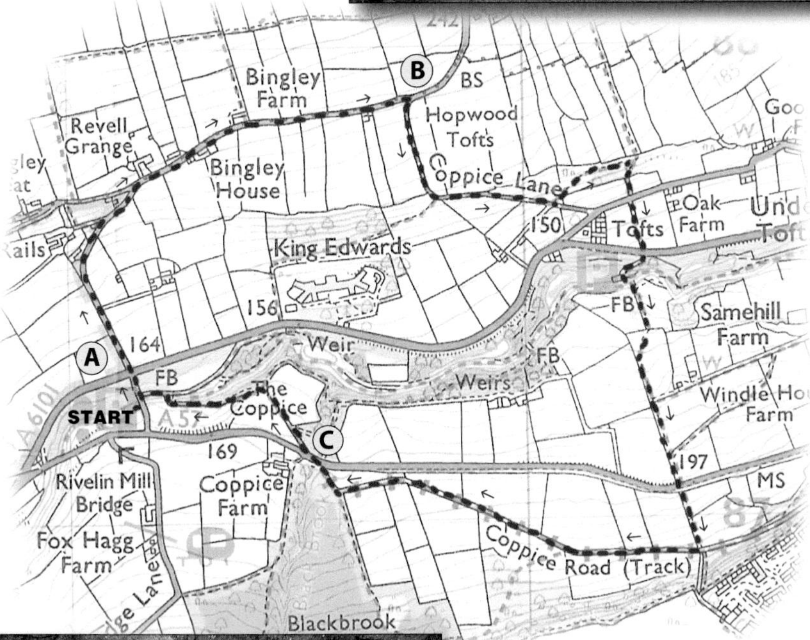

*View of Coppice Road (Track)*

Walk 14

# Lodge Moor

**Distance:** 3¼ Miles
**Approximate Time:** 2Hrs
**Parking:** Sportsman Inn car park
**Refreshments:** Sportsman Inn
**Description:** Not to be attempted after heavy rain.

**START: Sportsman Inn car park, Redmires Road.**

Set off from the car park along a vague path at right angles to the road. Walk alongside the football pitch towards a white-topped marker post and continue along the side of the wall to a gravel path.

Turn right along the conduit and continue to a road. Turn left to a footpath at the bend in the road, turn right and proceed to the edge of the dam. Fork right at the gate and immediately squeeze through the gap on the left at the side of the gate. Turn right alongside the fence and continue to a stone building, then turn left along the side of the dam. Almost at the top of a slight hill look for a path on the left across the water slipway between the two dams. Cross the slipway if passable and walk up to the edge of the next dam. Here turn left and continue along the path, veering left, to a gate at the corner of the first dam.

Turn half left and walk along the side of the wall for 15 yds.

Turn right at the corner and continue to the gate met earlier.

This time walk along the road facing you, past Soughley Cottage to a junction. Go straight on to a signed footpath on the left in the middle of a field wall, half way up a hill.

Turn left and walk straight across the field to a stile leading to the conduit. Cross the stile and turn left for 100 yds, then turn right at the bench and return to the start.

Soughley Cottage

Sportsman Inn, Redmires Road

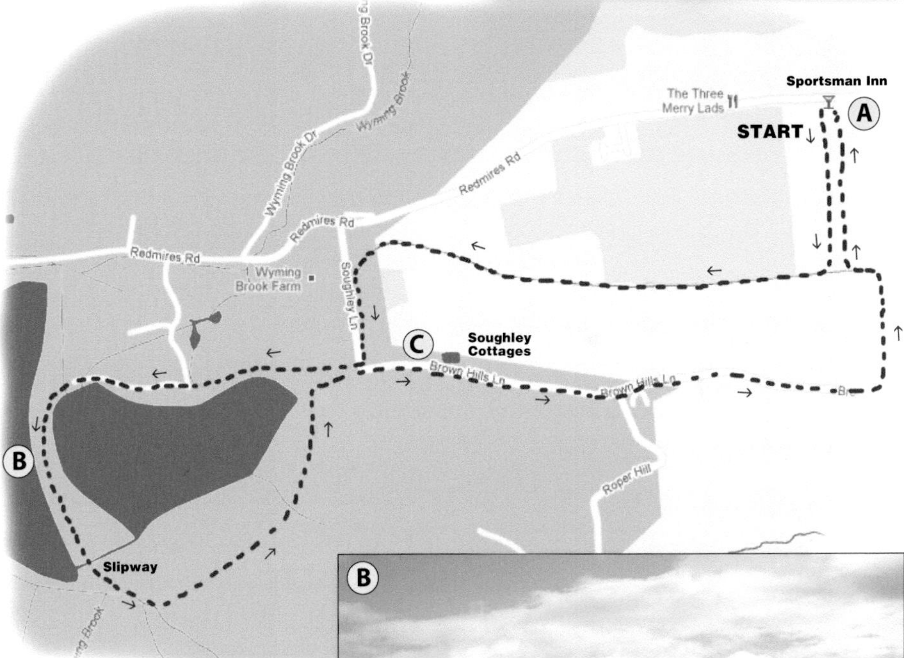

View over Redmires Dam

Walk 15

# Redmires Circuit

**Distance:** 3¾ Miles

**Approximate Time:** 2Hrs

**Parking:** Redmires car park

**Refreshments:** Three Merry Lads Pub, Redmires Road

**Description:** Pleasant moorland walk around all 3 dams.

**START: Redmires Car Park.**

Leave the car park via the main entrance, turn right and walk to the end of the road. Turn left at the gate and follow the path over two streams. Then cross a stile on the right and pass a Sheffield Water Works stone, passing it on its right.

Follow the path as marked by the posts, take a right fork at a boulder then veer left to a single tree. Continue on the path to cross a ladder stile (which can be seen from a distance) over a fence.

Then cross another ladder stile, this time over a wall, and continue down the path alongside the wall to its junction with a road. Here cross the stile, turn left and walk past the farm to a signpost and carved notice pointing to Fulwood Booth Farm. Follow this path through a metal gate and on to a signpost on the right. Turn right here and follow the path to a track, cross the stile and turn left.

Follow this track downhill to the lower dam and at the fork turn half left onto a gravel path. Walk along this to a path at the side of the gate and continue down to a junction with a private drive. Turn right past the houses to another drive on the left, turn along it to a path on the right just before a gate.

Walk along this path to a main road, turn left and walk back to the car park.

*View over Redmires Dam*

*Entrance to Moorland Path*

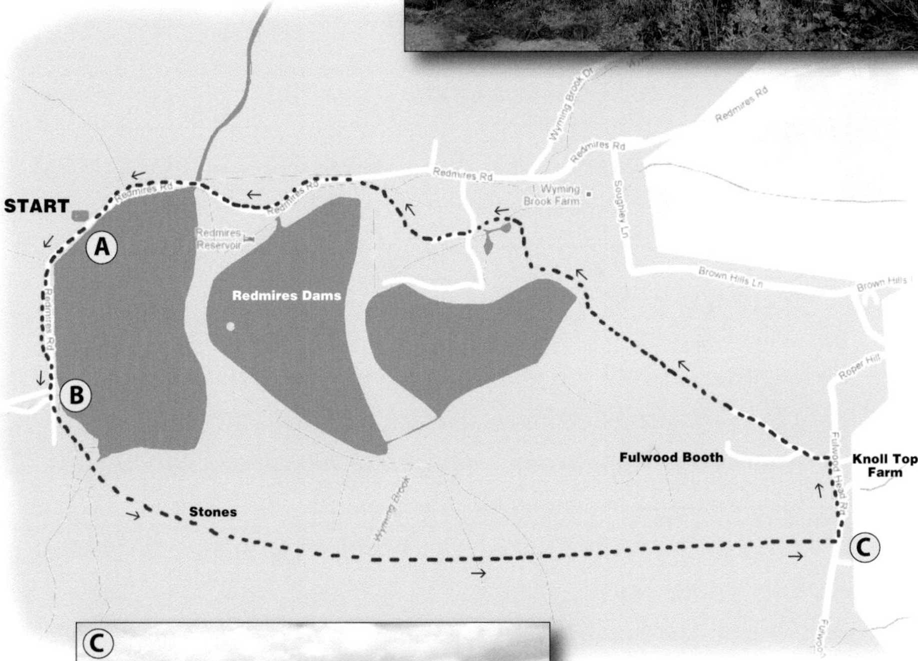

*View towards Fulwood*

Walk 16

# Totley Moss

**Distance:** 3 Miles

**Approximate Time:** 1½Hrs

**Parking:** Totley Hall Lane

**Refreshments:** Fleur-De-Lys Public House or Cricket Inn.

**Description:** Mainly walking on quite lanes but take care on Hillfoot Road.

**START: Fleur-De-Lys, Totley.**

Cross the main Baslow Road and proceed down Hillfoot Road opposite. After the school bear left down Chapel Lane and then take the cobbled path down a field to Penny Lane.

Here turn left and at the side of the "Cricket Inn" bear left diagonally across the sports field.

Turn left along the road and then right along Moss Road.

Go up this road until you reach a junction with a 'No Through Road' sign. Turn right here and follow the 'Public Byway' downhill.

When this path meets a road, turn right for 200 yds to a signpost on the left. Go down this stony path to cross an 'artificial brook' at the bottom, then in a further 100 yds go through a gap in the wall down to another, 'natural', brook.

Cross the bridge, turn right and follow the path to a gate. Through here and onto a lane, which you follow to a junction with a road.

At this junction turn right down a signed footpath. On meeting a drive, turn left to the junction with a road.

Turn right and continue back uphill to the Fleur-de-Lys.

Fleur-De-Lys Pub, Totley

View of Cricket Inn and the cricket ground

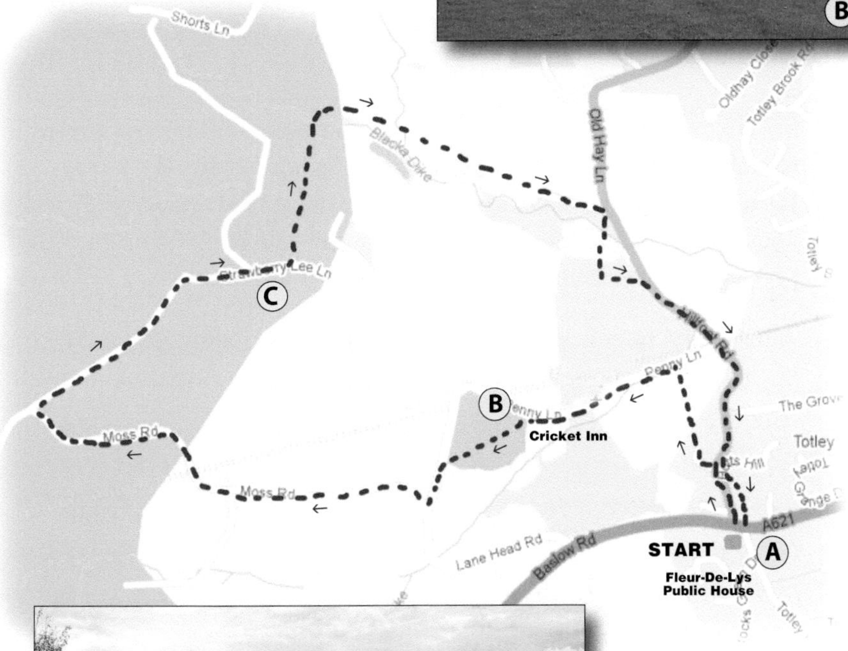

View over Sheffield

Walk 17

# Midhopestones

**Distance:** 3¾ Miles

**Approximate Time:** 2Hrs

**Parking:** Lay-by at Midhopestones

**Refreshments:** Ye Olde Mustard Pot, Public House

**Description:** Little know walk not far from Stocksbridge with excellent views towards Penistone.

**START: Midhopestones crossroads just over 1 mile from where the road through Stocksbridge joins the Stocksbridge By-pass.**
**Turn right at the crossroads onto a minor road signposted 'Penistone'. After 60 yds pass under the railway bridge to a lay-by on the left where you can park.**

Walk up the path from the lay-by to the disused railway line, 20 yds on the left from the lay-by. Turn left and walk along the path towards Sheffield until you reach the Fox Wire firm (1 mile).
Turn right down their drive to the by-pass, then turn left for 60 yds to a stile in the hedge. Cross it, then another stile and then a bridge.
Cross another stile then a wall and in 250 yds ascend some steps.
At the top turn left and then in 20 yds take the right fork towards a stile in the wall. Cross this and proceed towards a single tree 100 yds away.
Carry on up the hill, slightly left, to another stile in a wall by a stone milepost.
Cross it and walk straight across the field towards another stile near a small tree/bush over the wall.
Cross it and walk along the edge of the field with the wall on your left.
Cross another stile and walk along the edge of the next field past a huge mound of white farm material (? lime).

On reaching the road turn left, go over the crossroads and proceed for another 600 yds along the road to a signpost on the left.
Turn left here, walk up the farm drive past the farm and over a stile at the side of a gate. Carry on down the edge of several fields (and through a wood) to arrive back at the start.

*View of old railway bridge from lay-by*

*View of path along disused railway*

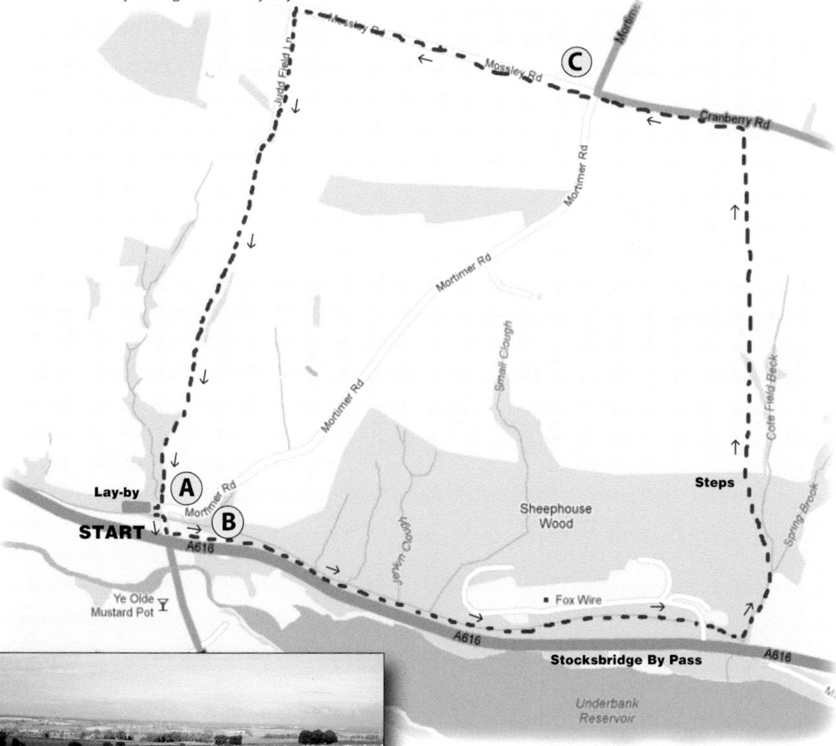

*View towards Penistone*

Walk 18

# More Hall Reservoir

**Distance:** 4 Miles
**Approximate Time:** 2Hrs
**Parking:** Eastern end of More Hall Reservoir
**Refreshments:** Picnic
**Description:** Some steep gradients overlooking the reservoir.

**START: The end of the embankment at the eastern end of the dam.**

Walk across the embankment and turn right along the dam for 100 yds. Here turn sharp left up first a path then a track to Brightholmlee.
Turn right then left at a stone signpost marked Bradfield. Follow the road to "Skye High Cottage" (1/2 mile) on the left and just after this cross a stile on the right. Walk up the field with the wall on your right, cross a stile then bear left to cross another.
Turn left along the walled track, then just before a farm turn left, descend and cross a stile to another track. Turn right and proceed uphill, passing through 2 gates and bearing right but passing to the left of some old quarry workings. At the end of the cutting bear right off the track and walk with a wall on your left.
The path becomes a trench then bear right towards a gate. Here cross the stile and go slightly right downhill to a track.
Go left along the track to where it bends left at a wooden stump.
Here turn RIGHT and descend diagonally across the field (no path) to cross a stile at the bottom right hand corner (hidden behind the trees).
Turn right along the lane to Snell House and opposite here turn left down some wooden steps.
Cross a footbridge and climb up the other side.

Water Tower

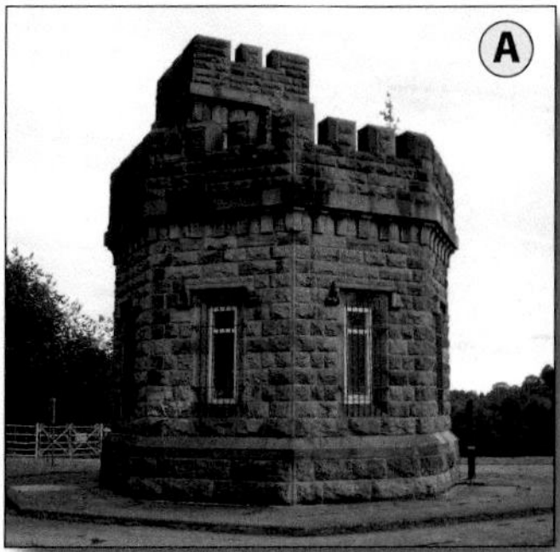


Cross another stile and then the corner of the field in the direction of the yellow arrow.

Three quarters of the way along the hedge is a stile, cross it and go diagonally left across the 'hump' to another stile.

Cross it into a lane and turn right. Proceed to the SECOND right hand bend and cross a stile at a signpost on the left. Keep straight ahead to join a road, turn right for 80 yds and then turn left through a gap in the fence.

Walk the few yards down to the dam, turn right and walk back to the start along the side of the dam.

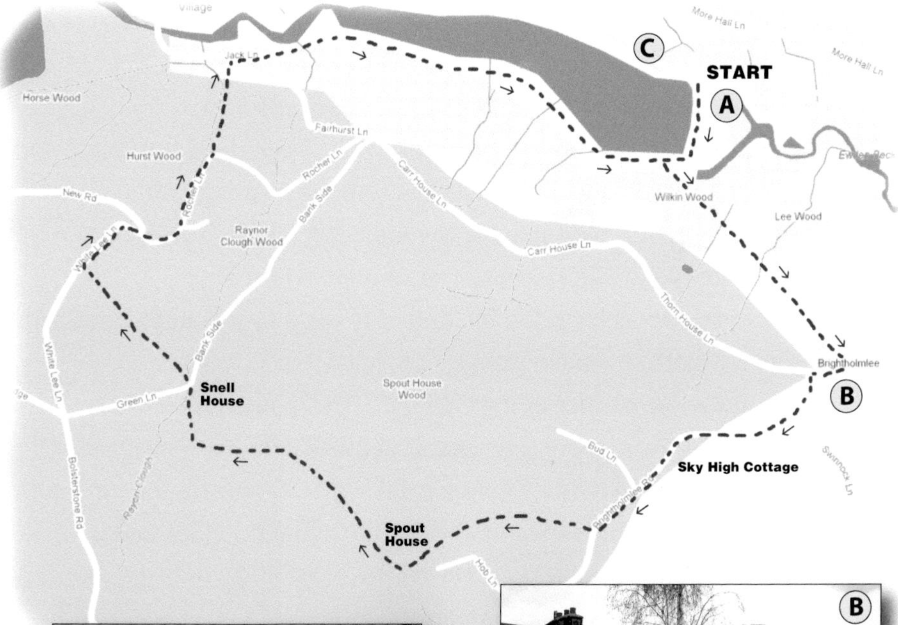

View across More Hall Reservoir

Cottage at Brightholmlee

Walk 19

# Rivelin Valley and Ronksley

**Distance:** 4 Miles

**Approximate Time:** 2¼Hrs

**Parking:** Rails Rd car park

**Refreshments:** Picnic spot near Rivelin Dam

**Description:** There is a steep climb from the stepping stones, which can be flooded after heavy rain.

**START: Rails Road, Car Park.**

Exit via the "back door", not the front car park entrance.
Follow the path and go up the steps to the main road, turn right and walk past the water works to where there are two signposts opposite each other on opposite sides of the road (1/4 mile).
Turn left and follow the path to the stepping stones.
Cross these, proceed up the hill and at the top of the steps turn right.
Follow the path to Rivelin Dam (1/2 mile).
Turn right and cross the embankment to the main road.
Turn left and walk to Onksley Lane (1/4 mile).
Turn right up the lane to Ronksley Hall Farm. Opposite the farm turn right along a country lane and proceed to a junction (3/4 mile).
Just before a farm turn right down the road and continue along it, turning left, to meet Rails Road, after 1/2 mile.
Turn right and walk down the road back to the car park, crossing another main road on the way.

*Reservoir at the far end of the car park*

*Rivelin Dam*

*View towards Lodge Moor*

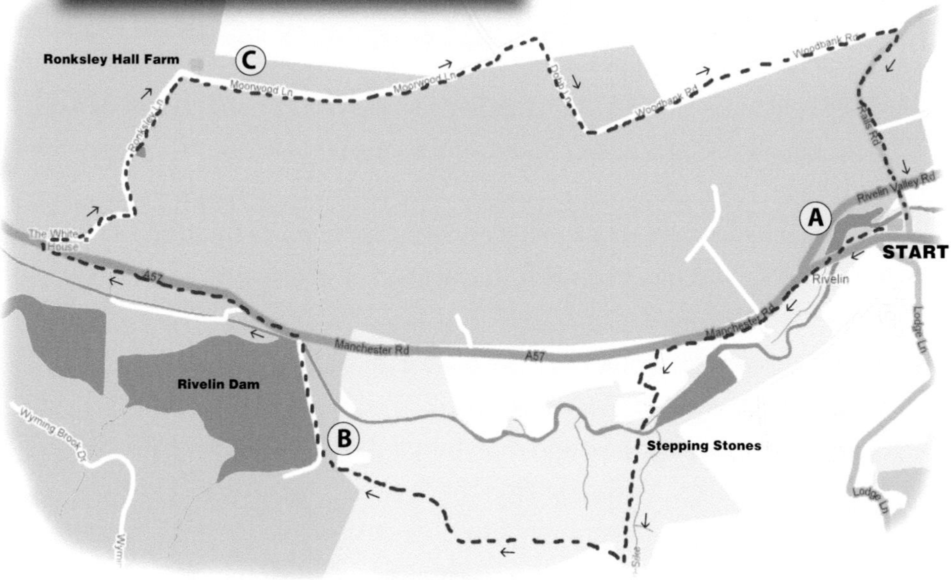

# Walk 20 Round House

**Distance:** 3 Miles
**Approximate Time:** 1½Hrs
**Parking:** Lay-by opposite Norfolk Arms Pub
**Refreshments:** Norfolk Arms Public House
**Description:** An easy moorland walk, with great views over the city.

**START: Lay-by opposite the Norfolk Arms pub.**

Walk down Sheephill Road at the side of the Round House to the junction with Houndkirk Road and fork right up the unmade road.
Proceed to the gate at the end of the plantation and turn right on the small path running round the edge of the plantation but outside the fence.
Follow this path until it reaches a wide, stoney track then turn right and proceed to Ringinglow Road.
Cross this main road and proceed on the path at right angles to the road up a slight hill towards a white marker sign.
Carry on and just over the top of the hill take the centre path.
This leads towards a wall and then veers left towards a stile in the wall.
Cross this and proceed along the 'walled lane' towards the farmyard.
Pass through here veering left and follow the track to Fulwood Lane.
Turn right and follow the road for half a mile to a signpost on the left past Greenhouse Lane.
Turn left at the signpost and then turn right, following the path round to the left to a signpost marking the Sheffield Round Walk.
Cross the bridge and go uphill, through a small car park and onto the road. Turn left and walk along to Ringinglow Rd, turn left and back to the start.

*Round House, Ringinglow*

*View towards Dore and Totley from Houndkirk Road*

*Rotary Club view finder on Greenhouse Lane*

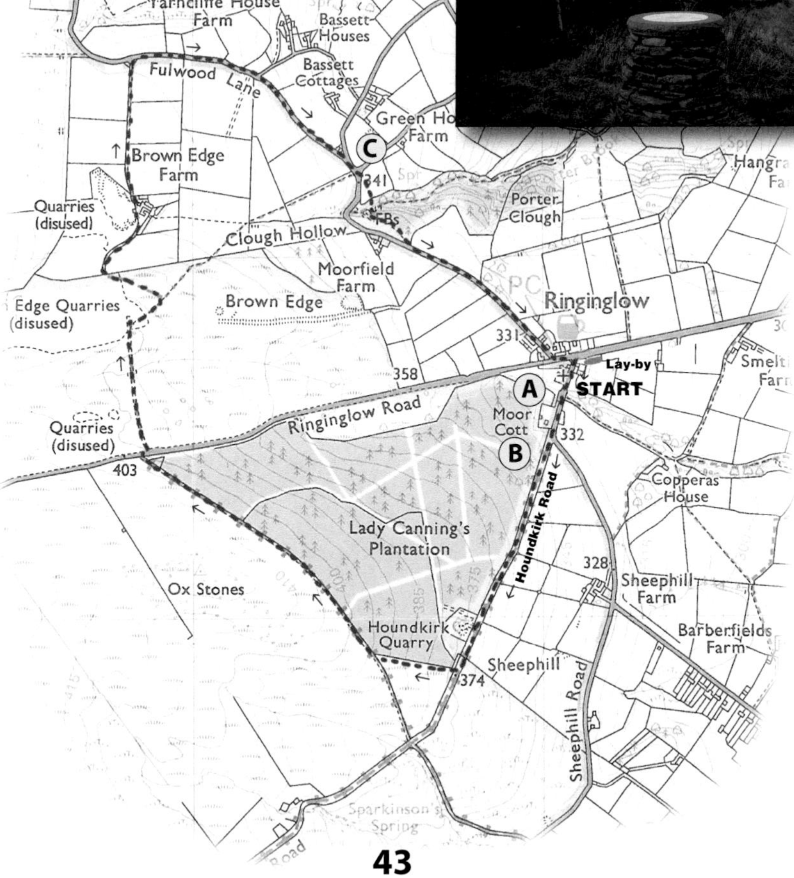

Walk 21

# Wyming Brook

**Distance:** 3 Miles

**Approximate Time:** 1½Hrs

**Parking:** Rivelin Dam Car Park

**Refreshments:** Picnic

**Description:** A moderate, varied walk. Watch your footing on the stretch alongside the brook.

**START: Car park at Lower Rivelin Dam.**

Turn left out of the car park and walk alongside the dam for 300 yds. Turn left up Wyming Brook (as per the wooden panel) and walk steeply to the top, following the woodland path alongside the brook.

Cross the stream on the stepping stones, turn left up some steps and turn right at the car park.

Go through a gate and immediately fork left as signposted by a wooden 'Woodcock' sign, not on the gravel path (Wyming Brook Drive).

Continue along the top of the woods and then after 500 yds the path begins a descent into the valley. Fork right here (at the Crossbill post) and continue down to a track.

Turn left and just after a double bend, the first part of which is a bridge across a stream, turn left at a council footpath sign and a tree split in two. Follow this sign, veering left and walk uphill to a fence.

Pass through the gate and walk uphill until it joins another path from the right, turn left and continue to a crossroad of paths (the Headstone is directly ahead). Turn right and walk downhill to a footbridge across a river. Go over the bridge and turn right to follow the path alongside the river to another bridge.

Turn right along a wide track, take a left fork further on and continue back to the start.

*Rivelin Dam Embankment*

*Entrance to Wyming Brook*

*View over Rivelin Dam*

Walk
22

# Carr Bridge (Fulwood)

**Distance:** 3½ Miles

**Approximate Time:** 2Hrs

**Parking:** Clough Lane just beyond Carr Bridge

**Refreshments:** Forge Dam Cafe

**Description:** An easy walk in the Mayfield Valley.

**START: Carr Bridge, down Quiet Lane from School Green Lane.**

Stand on the bridge with your back to School Green Lane.

Take the signed path on the left and then immediately the right fork (Bridleway). In 30 yds turn left and proceed to a signpost on the right.

Turn right through a gate and walk uphill to some steps and a stile.

Go over it and proceed diagonally left to another stile at the side of a gate. Go over this and follow the path to a road.

Turn left and in 300 yds turn right at a signpost opposite three terraced houses.

Climb the path to a ladder stile, go over it and continue straight ahead along a walled path to the main road (Ringinglow Road).

Turn left and in 20 yds turn right at the signpost at the side of the farm.

Proceed along the path and over a stile on the left and then along the side of the field.

Go over two more stiles and then at the third turn left. After 40 yds turn left again and follow the path round a clump of trees to a stile.

Turn right and at the next corner of the field turn left and follow this path to the pavilion.

Turn left along the access road and continue to the main road again.

Turn left for 100 yds, then turn right at the signpost and follow this path to a road.

Cross the road, proceed through the gateway and turn left immediately to a signpost in the bottom corner of the field.

Here turn left and exit onto the road, turn right and in 20 yds turn right at a signpost over a stone stile. Proceed down the field to a double stile and straight on to another two stiles and a lane. Turn left and carry straight on to meet a road. Turn left and go straight ahead at the next bend which is a bridleway.

After 150 yds turn right at an opening in the fence and follow this path, taking the left fork, back to the start.

*Carr Bridge on Quiet Lane*

*View over Mayfield Valley*

*Cottages on Cottage Lane*

Walk
23

# Wharncliffe Crags

**Distance:** 3 Miles
**Approximate Time:** 1½Hrs
**Parking:** Station Road, Deepcar
**Refreshments:** Picnic
**Description:** A mainly wooded walk with an interesting cliff top view

**START: Station Road, Deepcar.**

Walk along Station Road past Lowood WMC and cross the stone bridge. Turn left at the second signpost onto a stone track.
Follow the path through the woods through two railway tunnels and past a small dam. At a crossroads of paths go straight on to a larger dam and there take the path on its right (not a right turn).
Take the right fork at the edge of the woods and pass through a stile at the side of a gate.
Walk uphill on the grassy path until you reach the cliff edge.
Turn left and walk along the cliff top, passing through a gate.
Fork right and continue for half-a-mile to a wide junction of paths.
Turn right here and walk down to a fork just before a coniferous plantation.
Turn right again and proceed to a track. Where you turn right again and walk down to a wide track called Plank Gate, a medieval way out of Sheffield. Turn right yet again and continue to a fork.
Here fork left and follow the path through another railway tunnel.
Turn right and go past the old station to Station Rd and back to the start.

*Lowood WMC on Station Road*

*Railway Tunnel*

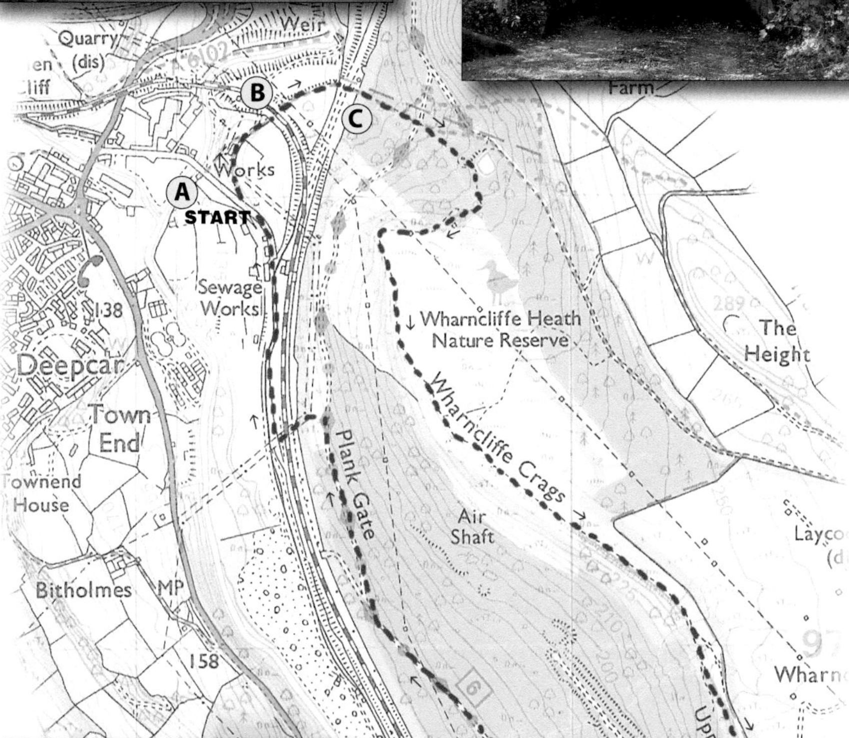

*Plank Gate*

# Walk 24 Crosspool

**Distance:** 3 Miles

**Approximate Time:** 1½Hrs

**Parking:** Stephen Hill Road

**Refreshments:** Crosspool Tavern

**Description:** Varied walk around Crosspool with splendid views.

**START: Junction of Manchester Road and Stephen Hill Road.**

Walk up Stephen Hill Road to Marsh Lane, turn left and proceed to the second signpost on the right at a barrier (100 yds).

Turn right and follow the path to a stile, go over it and fork right.

Walk downhill to a gap in the wall and pass through it to another wall gap by a gate.

Pass through this and cross the field diagonally to a stile in the bottom corner. Cross this, the one with a green disc, and follow the path for a 100 yds to a crossroads of paths.

Turn left and proceed downhill to Bolehill Road, then turn left for 100 yds to a wide drive on the right.

Go through the bridleway barrier and veer left on the path through the allotments to Hagg Hill. Go straight across and follow the path to a gateway in a wall, turn left and go uphill to Long Lane.

Go straight across again through the barrier to a fork. Fork right to a crossroads of paths (15 yds), turn right and go downhill (not over stile) to Long Lane.

Turn left and walk along flat Hagg Lane, ignoring the left turn uphill. Continue for 300 yds to a bridleway signpost at two stone gateposts on the left. Turn left and follow the path uphill to the corner of the stonewall and proceed alongside the wall to a sharp left hand bend.

Here turn right along a path and walk uphill, again round a left hand bend. At the top of the hill go straight on alongside the wall to Hagg Lane and then turn left for 100 yds to a path on the right with a barrier. Go through the barrier and follow the path to a crossroads of paths. Turn right and proceed uphill (ignoring a path on the left) to another crossroads of paths.

Here turn left, then left again and immediately right, walking through the allotments to Back Lane.

Go straight across and along Clough Fields. On reaching the stables turn right along the drive and then left at the water trough.

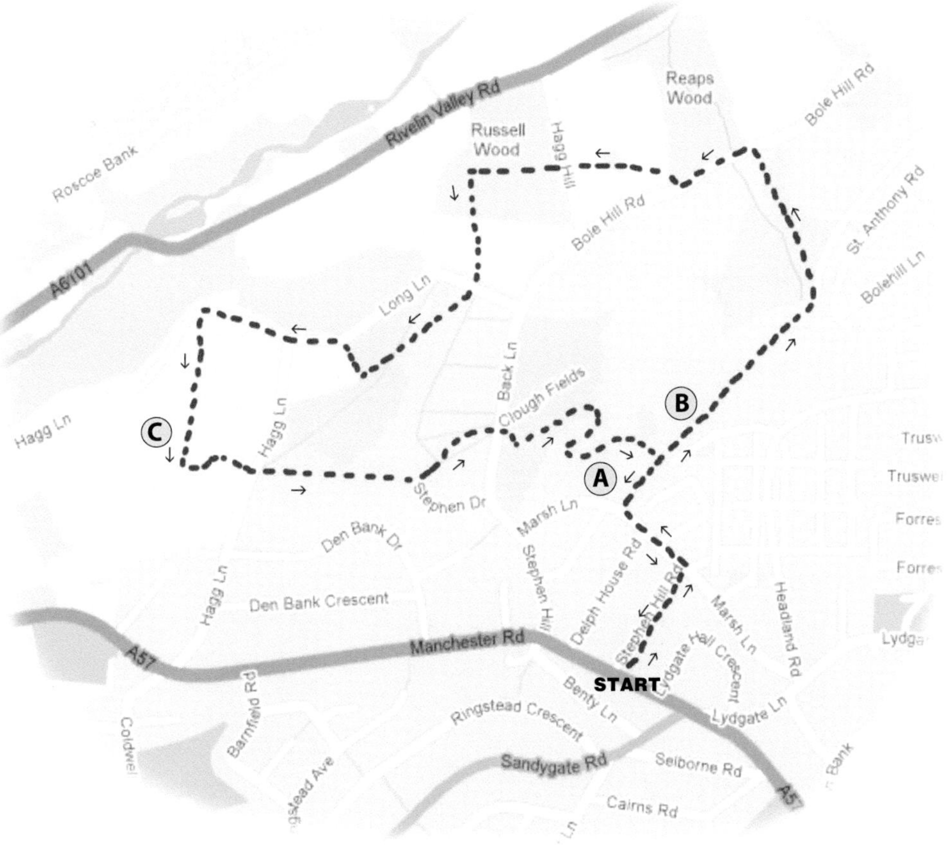

Then turn right and then left along a walled path.
At the signpost climb four steps and a stile, turn left and after a few yards fork right. Follow the path to double signposts at the side of a wall, cross the stile and proceed along the path to the road.
Turn left to Stephen Hill Road, turn right and go back to the start.

*View over Clough Fields*

*View towards Hillsborough*

*View over Stannington*